Contents

Symbols used in this guide

─────────

Outlines of Roman walls
(still visible)

═════════

Outlines of Roman walls
(no longer visible)

─────────

Outlines of Iron Age Town
(no longer visible)

Q Town Wall ▶

Roman points of interest
(still visible)

Temple ▶

Roman points of interest
(no longer visible)

Market ▶

Iron Age point of interest
(no longer visible)

The Winchester City Museum
(The Venta Belgarum gallery)

NASA

Winchester looking north, 250 CE.

Introduction

Winchester has a long and complex history, spanning more than two thousand years. Today it is a thriving city dominated by Winchester Cathedral. This guide explores how Winchester evolved from 30 CE to 350 CE. In this time it changed from a centre for the local *Atrebates* tribe to a prosperous Roman town. After this date the Roman Empire started a gradual decline and by 410 CE Britain was under constant attack by marauding Anglo-Saxons. Hundreds of years later Winchester would become the main centre for *Alfred the Great's* network of defended towns which ultimately led to the defeat of the Vikings.

The guide features full-colour 3D maps all looking north *(unless specified otherwise)*, reconstructions of mosaics and artefacts. Detailed maps show where each site or artefact is in present-day Winchester.

Towns and cities

The Romans defined towns and cities differently to how we do in the present day. They had three main types of town:

- *A Colonia, which was a rough equivalent of a city.*
- *A Municipium, which was slightly less important than a colonia.*
- *A Civitas capital, which was a broad equivalent of a large market town.*

The Romans called Pre-Roman towns 'oppida'.

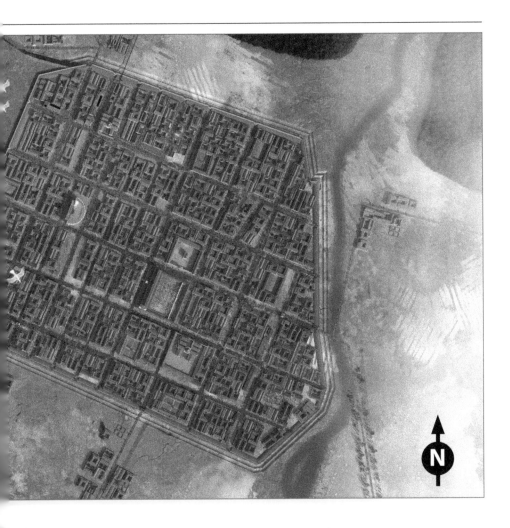

The Romans

The city of Rome in central Italy was formed around 800 BCE and grew over the centuries into the Roman Empire, which covered most of Europe and northern Africa. It was a highly sophisticated and technologically advanced society, with a huge army, major roads and large cities.

Britain at that time was a mysterious place with fierce tribes and valuable metals, which became the focus of an attempted invasion in 55 BCE and 54 BCE by *Julius Caesar*.

Those invasions were repelled by local tribes and the Romans did not try again to invade Britain for almost 100 years.

By 43 CE the *Emperor Claudius (who needed the army's support)* decided to invade Britain, which was weakened by the death of *King Cunobelin* of the *Trinovantes*, who lived in *Camulodunum (Colchester)*. After attacking Colchester his forces then moved across England including where present day Winchester is located...

Visiting Winchester

Winchester lies about 68 miles (109 km) south -west of London. The Winchester City Museum (The Venta Belgarum gallery), close to Winchester Cathedral has mosaics, artefacts and more found in Winchester. Most Roman sites mentioned in this book are no longer visible, apart from a small section of the south-east section of the Roman Wall.

Oram's Arbour

Hillfort

Defensive ditch

Line of future Roman Town Wall

Winchester, looking north, 70 BCE.

Winchester 70 BCE

Winchester had long been occupied before the Roman invasion and had strong ties with continental Europe. Around 150 BCE *Belgic*[1] tribes occupied the lands of local British tribes in the south, having three main centres in Winchester, Chichester and Silchester *(a village near Basingstoke)*. These tribes became the *Atrebates* and kept trade links with the continent. A small settlement, now known as *Oram's Arbour,* was established around 100 BCE in the area of Winchester indicated by the green line on the map. Although it was possibly abandoned 50 years later. It may have functioned like a market, with people living in small hillforts to the south of Winchester. Probably due to their connections with Europe, the Atrebates began to trade with the Romans, which would help them later on...

1. Pre-Roman tribes who lived in the Belgium, France and Luxembourg area.

Find out more
There are Iron Age artefacts or display in the Winchester City Museum (The Venta Belgarum gallery).

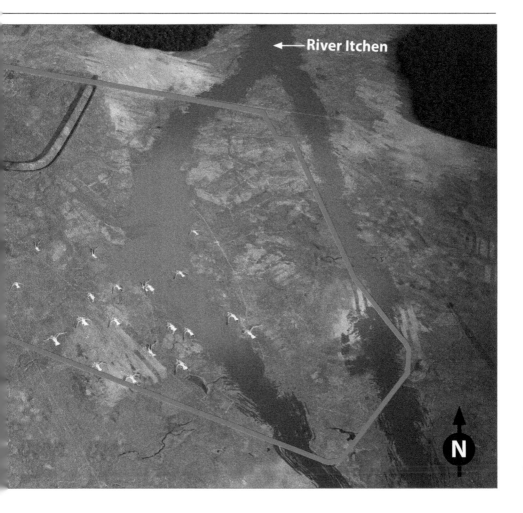

River Itchen

N

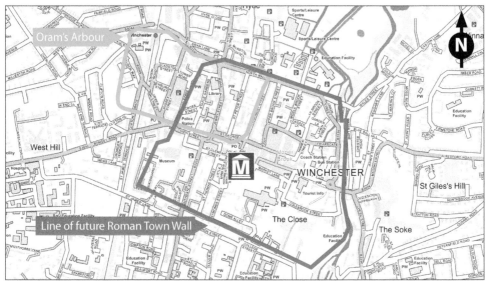

Oram's Arbour

Line of future Roman Town Wall

N

Contains Ordnance Survey data © Crown copyright and database right 2024

Abandoned hillfort

Site of Oram's Arbour

Civitas[1]

Basic defences under construction

Line of future Roman Town Wall

Winchester, looking north, 70 CE.

Winchester 70 CE

In 43 CE the Romans invaded southern Britain focusing their initial efforts on *Camulodunum (Colchester)* before moving west. The local *Atrebates* already had dealings with the Romans and did not oppose their presence, which may explain why no Roman fort has yet been found. In most other examples a Roman town would have originally started as a fort, as the area would need to be defended from hostile locals. Around 70 CE the Romans established a *civitas*[1] called *Venta Belgarum*[2], with the main capital *(at the time)* centred on Chichester 43 miles *(69 km)* to the south east.

1. A Civitas was a broad equivalent of a large market town.
2. Venta Belgarum means 'The market place of the Belgae'.[3]
3. The Belgae were pre-Roman tribes who lived in the area which is now Belgium, France and Luxembourg.

Find out more

There are no visible Roman remains of the early Roman town, except for the River Itchen. The river was later actually diverted by the Romans to allow them to establish the town (see overleaf), as previously the river flowed further to the west. Note how the defences do not yet encircle the whole town, as they would not be completed until the late 2nd century.

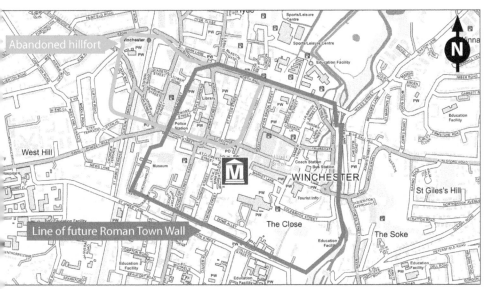

Abandoned hillfort

West Hill

WINCHESTER

St Giles's Hill

The Close

The Soke

Line of future Roman Town Wall

Winchester, looking north, 190 CE.

Winchester 190 CE

By the late 2nd century the whole of *Venta Belgarum* was defended by a earthworks and wooden pallisades[1]. In addition the River Itchen had been diverted, to allow more room for building. Not much is known about the types of buildings that *Venta Belgarum* had, although it probably followed the patterns of other similar sized Roman towns. For example many Roman towns had amphitheatres to entertain the locals, along with temples and theatres. One building known to exist was the Basilica, which was surrounded by a Forum, acting as the governmental and economic hub of *Venta Belgarum (see page 18)*. Most of the houses may have been built from wood and were gradually upgraded as the years passed. Evidence for an aqueduct which supplied the town with water has been found, although where exactly it was located is still not known.

1. Wooden walls with stakes on the top.

Find out more

There are no visible remains of the defensive earthworks, as they were later built over. However the present day street plan follows much of th original Roman street plan.

Some of the buildings shown have been found by archaeologists, while others (marked*) are speculative, but have been found in other Roman towns.

Diverted River Itchen

Theatre*

Temple

Basilica/Forum *(See page 18)*

Public Bathhouse*

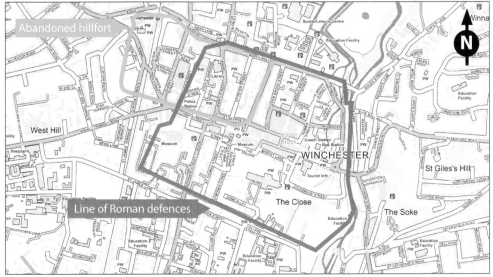

Abandoned hillfort

West Hill

WINCHESTER

St Giles's Hill

The Soke

The Close

Line of Roman defences

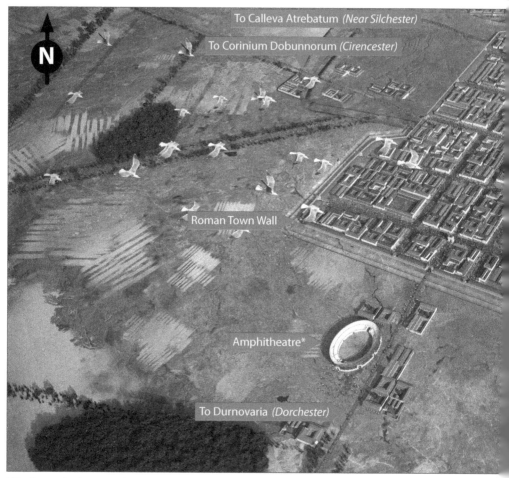

To Calleva Atrebatum *(Near Silchester)*

To Corinium Dobunnorum *(Cirencester)*

Roman Town Wall

Amphitheatre*

To Durnovaria *(Dorchester)*

Winchester looking north, 250 CE.

Winchester 250 CE

By this time the wooden defences had been strengthened with stone replacements. *Venta Belgarum* was the fifth largest town in Roman Britain. It was surrounded by a network of smaller towns and villages producing items such as building materials, housewares and jewellery.

Items from across the Roman Empire have been found in Winchester, some from as far away as Egypt and Cyprus. Public and private buildings were upgraded to more durable stone versions. Some of the citizens grew so wealthy they could afford villas in the surrounding countryside, such as at *Sparsholt (see page 28).*

After the Romans

Winchester and probably its Roman defences would form a key part of (King) Alfred the Great's strategy to defend southern Britain against the Vikings around 600 years later.

Find out more

Most of the Roman wall is lost or obscured by Saxon or medieval walls, except for a small south-eastern section. Extensive examples of mosaics and artefacts can be seen in the Winchester City Museum (The Venta Belgarum gallery).

Some of the buildings shown have been found by archaeologists, while others (marked*) are speculative, but have been found in other Roman towns.

Aqueduct*

Theatre*

Temple of Epona *(See page 26)*

Temple

Basilica/Forum *(See page 18)*

Public Bathhouse*

Granary*

Town Wall

To Noviomagus Reginorum *(Chichester)*

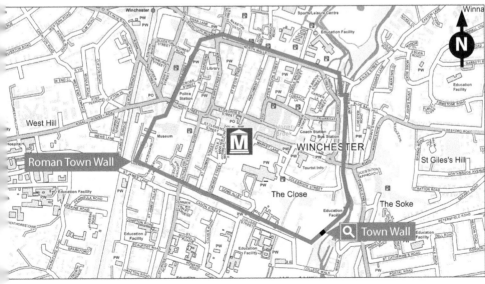

Winchester

Sports/Leisure Centre

Education Facility

N

Education Facility

West Hill

Roman Town Wall

M

WINCHESTER

St Giles's Hill

The Close

The Soke

Town Wall

Westgate

Southgate (see page 16)

The Roman Town Wall, looking north, 250 CE.

The Roman Town Wall

Unlike many other towns in Roman Britain, *Venta Belgarum* was in relatively peaceful territory, so defences seem not to have been a high priority. A basic earthwork defence system was built around 50 CE with wooden defences.

Around 190 CE the earthwork defence system circled the entire town, although another 20-30 years would pass until the defences were upgraded with stone. The Town Wall was possibly about 5 metres *(16.4 feet)* high and around 3 metres *(9.8 feet)* thick. Around the wall there were at least five gatehouses and many towers guarded by centurions, legionaries and auxiliaries. The main image also shows how the Town Wall was a continuous circuit, so that troops could move to any part rapidly.

Most of the Roman gatehouses were demolished in the last few hundred years, Kingsgate is now covered by a medieval gatehouse.

Find out more

Most of the Roman Wall is no longer visible, having been destroyed or incorporated into later medieval walls. One small section can be seen on the inner facing wall at the Pilgrims School playing field. Small parts of Roman wall mixed with later wall can also be seen on the outer south-east walls. None of the Roman Gatehouses are visible although detailed models can be seen in the Winchester City Museum (The Venta Belgarum gallery).

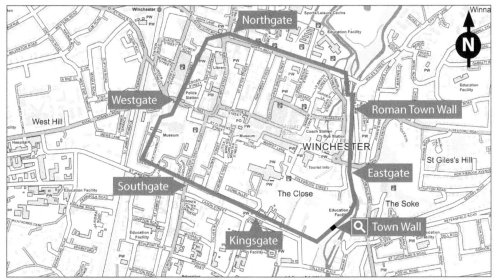

Site of Southgate, looking north, 190 CE.

Southgate 190 CE

Venta Belgarum's Southgate was set back into earthwork defences and covered the road which possibly led to Durnovaria (Dorchester[1]). The Eastgate may have led to Noviomagus Reginorum (Chichester), with the Northgate leading to Calleva Atrebatum (Silchester, a village near Basingstoke). This left the Westgate which led eventually to Corinium Dobunnorum (Cirencester). All of these towns, except Corinium Dobunnorum were part of the Atrebates territory, with the last town part of the Dobunni tribe's territory. Above the gatehouses centurions, legionaries and auxiliaries would have defended the town, using round stones and javelins.

1. There were other smaller locations along the Roman roads, but the ones mentioned were the next large town on from Venta Belgarum.

Find out more

There are no surviving remains of the wooden gatehouse. There is a detailed model of the wooden Southgate in Winchester City Museum (The Venta Belgarum gallery).

Southgate

Defensive earthworks

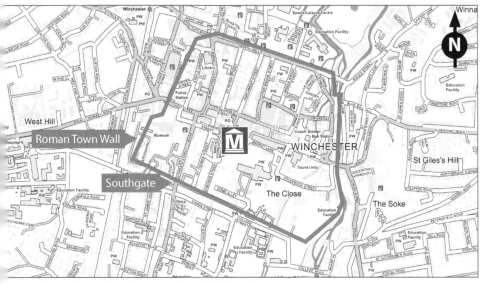

Roman Town Wall

Southgate

Roman Town Wall

Southgate

Site of Southgate, looking north, 250 CE.

Southgate 250 CE

By the early 3rd century the defences surrounding V*enta Belgarum* had been upgraded with stone replacements. As mentioned before, this would have been more for cosmetic reasons, rather than responding to a specific threat. The new design was built *into* the Town Wall, rather than projecting *out* of it. The Romans were continuously evolving and experimenting with their town defences, probably as a result of their vast experience of defending and attacking sites all across the Roman Empire. We can imagine that if someone tried to attack the town, the deep double ditches would have forced the attackers to attack the gatehouses. The gatehouses themselves acted as funnels, drawing the attackers in under constant defensive fire from stones and spears. If somehow the attackers got through all that, they still had to breach the huge wooden gates and by then reinforcements from other towns would be on the way!

Find out more

There are no surviving remains of the stone gatehouse. There is a detailed model of the stone Southgate in Winchester City Museum (The Venta Belgarum gallery).

Some of the buildings shown have been found by archaeologists, while others (marked*) are speculative, but have been found in other Roman towns.

Triumphal Arch*

Southgate

Market stalls*

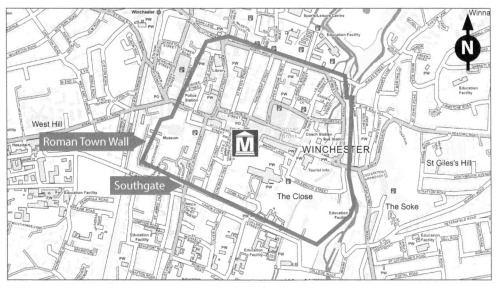

Roman Town Wall

Southgate

Contains Ordnance Survey data © Crown copyright and database right 2024

The site of the Basilica and Forum, looking north, 250 CE.

The Basilica and Forum

The Basilica and Forum *(public square)* were the most important civic structures in major Roman towns. The Basilica was the commercial and administrative heart of Roman Winchester, and was where deals were made and laws practised; it was also the regional government office. Large statues would have dominated the Forum where the population of the local area could meet. Various offices for local administrators and merchants surrounded the Forum, which would have had a colonnade providing shade in summer and shelter in winter. There would also have been market stalls selling food and household items sourced from all over the Roman Empire. Some of the merchants who traded here became very rich and built large villas in the surrounding countryside, such as Sparsholt Villa *(shown on page 28)*. A *macellum* (meat market)* may have stood near to the Basilica, like one found at St.Albans.

Find out more

Much of the Basilica and Forum is hidden beneath Winchester Cathedral and the Wessex Hotel. Its exact location is not certain, but a large public building complex was excavated in this area in the 1960s, dating from around the end of the first century.
The exact layout of the site is not known, so a possible arrangement is shown on the main image and map. Archaeologists believe they may also have found a temple complex, as shown above.

Temple

Forum

Macellum*

N

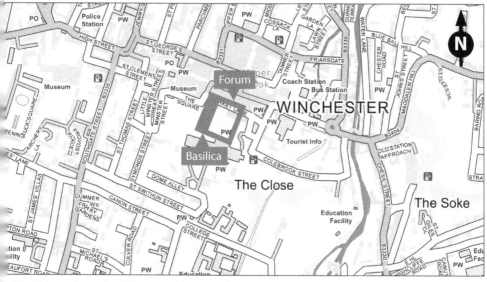

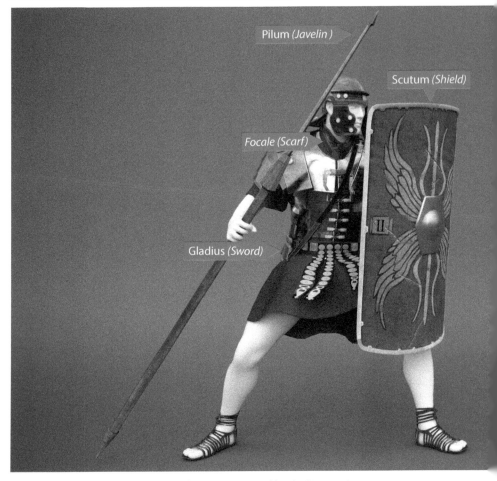

Pilum *(Javelin)*

Scutum *(Shield)*

Focale *(Scarf)*

Gladius *(Sword)*

A view showing typical weapons and equipment used by the Roman Army.

The Roman Army

Typically when the Roman Army moved into a new area in Britain, they would form a travelling camp called a *castra*. This could be built quickly, while under attack from local tribes. Then if required a much larger wooden fortress would be constructed. Often the fortress would be slowly converted into a civilian town. Winchester is quite unusual that no evidence of a military fortress has yet been found. The local *Atrebates* tribe was known to be pro-Roman, so perhaps this meant that a fortress was not required. However the Romans[1] didn't leave the town undefended, as defences were built and manned by the Roman Army. It also seems likely that army engineers were involved in re-routing the River Itchen, which would have involved significant skill and equipment to achieve.

1. *Colchester had been left undefended, until Boudica and 120,000 warriors burnt it to the ground.*

Find out more

There are models showing the military defences built by the Roman Army at the Winchester City Museum (The Venta Belgarum gallery).

It is thought that the Legio II Augusta (Second Legion Augustus) was the first part of the Roman Army to enter the area where Winchester now stands. It is not known which legion rerouted the River Itchen.

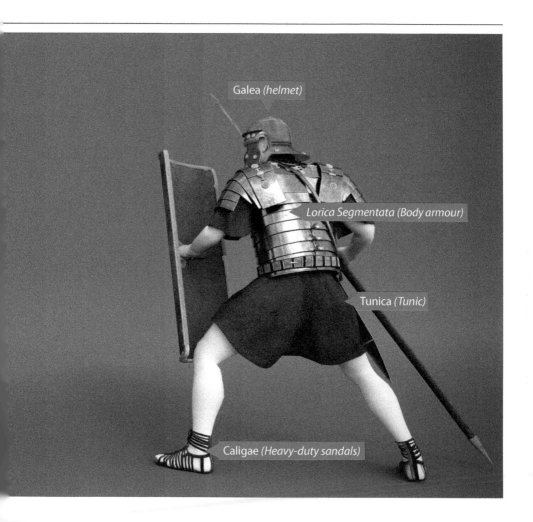

Galea *(helmet)*

Lorica Segmentata *(Body armour)*

Tunica *(Tunic)*

Caligae *(Heavy-duty sandals)*

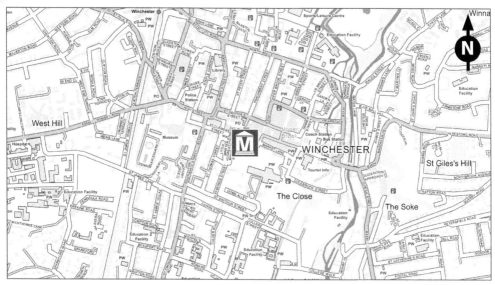

Painted walls

Venus

Possible interior of the building which housed the Floral Mosaic, around 220 CE.

The Floral Mosaic

The Floral Mosaic was found at The Brooks as part of an archaeological dig in 1987. Most Roman mosaics used complex interweaving patterns, now known as *guilloche*, which were thought to represent infinity. It is possible that the Romans used mosaic pattern books to choose designs, then once a design was chosen it would be assembled onsite. The artist sometimes used flourishes such as red marks to tell others who had produced the mosaic.
Lotus flowers were often associated with *Venus*[1], although this particular design has not been found anywhere else in the western Roman Empire. It may have featured a depiction of *Venus* in the centre, like other mosaics found in Roman Britain.

1. *Venus was the Roman goddess of love (originally the Greek goddess Aphrodite).*

Find out more
Part of the Floral Mosaic and wall paintings can be seen at the Winchester City Museum (The Venta Belgarum gallery). Note the centre showing a depiction of Venus is speculative, but has been found in other mosaics in Roman Britain, such as one on display at Cirencester. Many wealthy homeowners had elaborate wall paintings, these ones are based on ones found in Rome.

Guilloche

Lotus flower

view showing how much of the mosaic can be seen in the present day.

A view showing how the Dragon Mirror may have looked around 150 CE.

The Dragon Mirror

In the 1970s archaeologists unearthed a set of religious artefacts in Victoria Road, including a copper alloy Dragon Mirror. This style of Dragon Mirror[1] is typically associated with northern tribes such as the *Brigantes*, rather than in the south of England. Dragons were used in art long before the start of the Roman Empire, with Roman versions influenced by countries on the eastern side of the empire including ancient Greece.

1. Note the red semi-precious gems shown are speculative, but may have once been part of the mirror. In Carlisle archaeologists found multiple semi-precious gems thought to have been part of rings. The gems had been glued in with vegetable glue which melted in the heat of a public bathhouse and were lost. In a similar way, semi-precious gems could have been lost from the mirror hundreds of years in the past.

Find out more

The Dragon Mirror is on display in the Winchester City Museum (The Venta Belgarum gallery).
Note the reflection in the mirror shows a fashionable hairstyle from the Roman Empire.

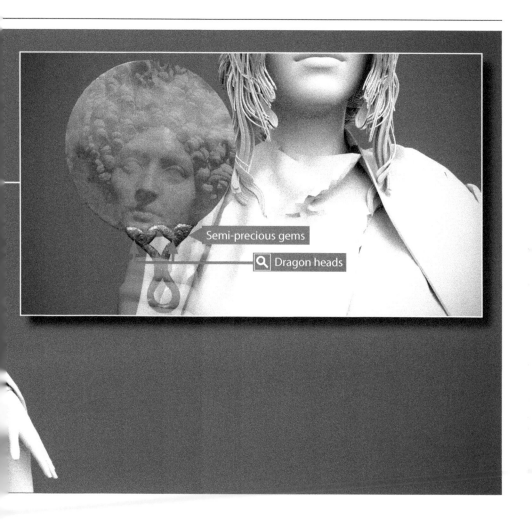

Semi-precious gems

🔍 Dragon heads

A view showing how the Dragon Mirror looks now.

Basilica

Temple

Temple of Epona, looking north.

*A possible view of the Temple of Epona around 250 CE, looking **west**.*

The Temple of Epona

Archaeologists discovered the remains of a small temple, later thought to be dedicated to *Epona*[1], in Lower Brook Street around 1966. The temple, built around 100 CE, replaced earlier wooden buildings and was itself replaced by a workshop around 290 CE. Roman temples in Britain typically follow two main designs, one rectangular[4] and the other called Romano-Celtic, which is the style/design of this temple.

1. *Epona was a Gallo-Roman[2] goddess who protected horses and was also associated with fertility.*
2. *Gallo-Roman was a fusion of the Gallic[3] and Roman religions. The Romans often incorporated local religions into their own, rather than simply enforcing theirs on to others.*
3. *Gallic people lived in mainland Europe, during the Iron Age and the Roman period.*
4. *See page 18 for an example of a rectangular temple.*

Find out more

Archaeologists discovered the remains of a small temple, later thought to be dedicated to Epona, in Lower Brook Street. There are no visible remains of the temple, but a small statuette, found next to the temple, is on display in the Winchester City Museum (The Venta Belgarum gallery). Some of the buildings shown have been found by archaeologists, while others (marked*) are speculative, but have been found in other Roman towns.

Theatre*

Public Bathhouse*

Temple of Epona

N

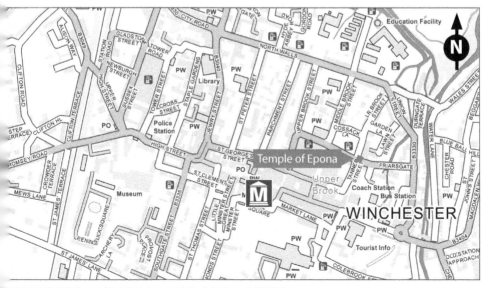

Sparsholt Villa, looking north around 350 CE.

Sparsholt Villa

In 1965 archaeologists uncovered a large villa at Sparsholt, 4 miles *(6 km)* west of Winchester. It is thought to have been built around 150 CE and then extended into a much larger building around 320 CE. Sparsholt Villa would have been at the centre of a large and prosperous farm estate. Its owners were probably wealthy merchants or perhaps important members of the local *Atrebates* tribe who had adopted the Roman way of life. Farm estates were made up of a number of smaller settlements farmed by tenant farmers, who would have provided the villa owners with a substantial income. Sparsholt Villa would have been self-sufficient, with its own kitchen garden for vegetables, an orchard growing fruit and nut varieties introduced by the Romans, such as plums and walnuts, a vineyard and a flower garden. Around the villa there would have been barns, granaries and a watermill for milling the estate's wheat.

Find out more

There are no visible remains o the villa at Sparsholt.
A reconstruction of part of the main building can be seen at Butser Ancient Farm, Petersfield, 20 miles (32 km) east of Winchester.
Winchester City Museum (The Venta Belgarum gallery) has a number of artefacts fro Sparsholt Villa, including a square mosaic, wall paintings and the remains of stone columns.
See overleaf for details of the Sparsholt Villa Mosaic.

Sparsholt Villa Mosaic[1]

Sparsholt Villa

Barn

Courtyard

Well

Bathhouse

Sparsholt Villa looking *west* in 350 CE.

Orchard

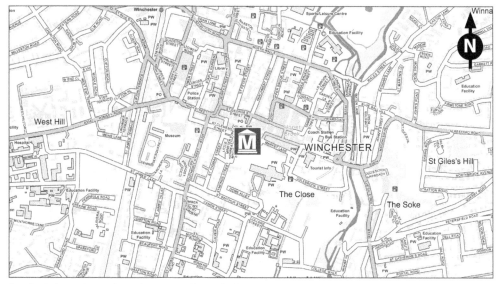

Guilloche

Guilloche

Scallop shells

Cantharus vess

Possible interior of the room which housed the Sparsholt Villa Mosaic, around 350 CE.

The Sparsholt Villa Mosaic

The Sparsholt Villa Mosaic, dating from the 4th century, was found by archaeologists in 1965, in the main reception room of the villa. The mosaic shares similar features with other mosaics found in Britain which were dedicated to the goddess *Venus*. In the centre there is a lotus flower *(or possibly a star)*, surrounded by waves and interlocking patterns thought to represent eternity[1]. In the corners are scallop shells *(another symbol of Venus)* and *canthari*, which were two handled drinking vessels. The elite of Romano-British society were highly educated and would have known the meaning of all the symbolism displayed in their mosaics. Mosaics in Roman Britain tended to show mythological and hunting scenes, unlike ones in the rest of the empire which tended to show scenes from wars.

1. *Now known as guilloche.*

Find out more

The Winchester City Museum (The Venta Belgarum gallery) has the Sparsholt Villa Mosaic on permanent display. There are also wall paintings and the remains of stone columns from Sparsholt Villa.

view showing how much of the mosaic can be seen in the present day.

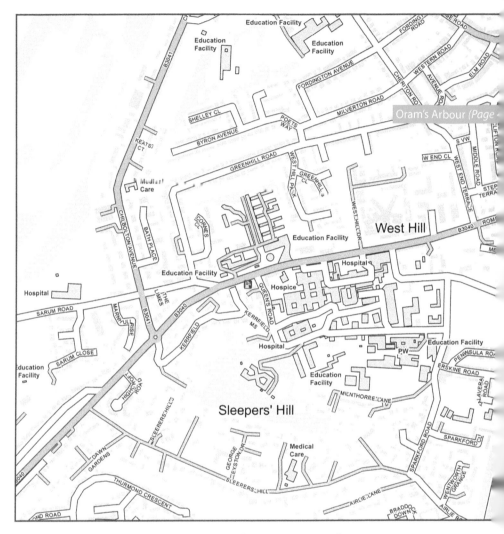

Roman Winchester today

Most of *Venta Belgarum* is now no longer visible, except for a small section of the Roman Wall. The Winchester City Museum *(The Venta Belgarum gallery)* has an extensive range of Roman mosaics, artefacts and displays. The red lines show where the original Roman walls were and the black lines show where partial Roman walls can still be seen. The blue squares shows post-Roman gatehouses. The sites shown on this map are also explored in more detail in the main part of this book, as well as showing the location of Winchester City Museum, which features Roman artefacts. All the exterior images of *Venta Belgarum* face north *(unless shown otherwise)*, so that you can compare the past with the present day maps.

This guide also shows how Sparsholt Villa, 4 miles (6 km) west of Winchester looked in Roman times. A mosaic from the villa can be seen at the Winchester City Museum (The Venta Belgarum gallery).

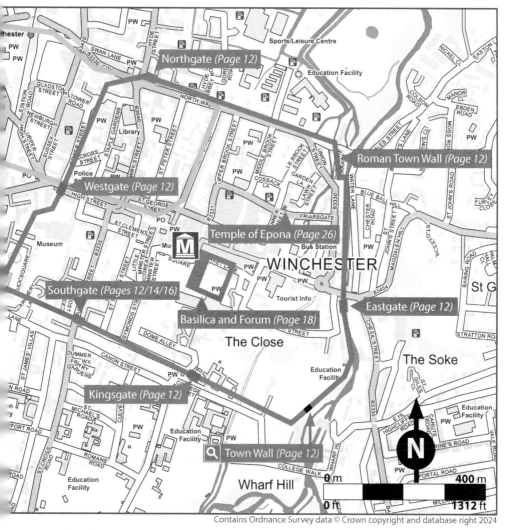

Symbols used on this map

———
Outlines of Roman Walls
(still visible)

———
Outlines of Roman Walls
(no longer visible)

===
Outlines of Iron Age Town
(no longer visible)

▬▬
Post-Roman gatehouses
(still visible)

[🔍 Town Wall *(Page 12)*]
Roman points of interest
(still visible)

[Eastgate *(Page 12)*]
Roman points of interest
(no longer visible)

[Oram's Arbour *(Page 4)*]
Iron Age point of interest
(no longer visible)

The Winchester City Museum
(the Venta Belgarum gallery):
The Floral Mosaic *(Page 22)*
Sparsholt Villa *(Page 28)*
Sparsholt Villa Mosaic
(Page 30)

First published January 2024
ISBN 978-1-7391254-4-8 *(Paperback)*
First Edition

Designed and published by JC3DVIS
www.jc3dvis.co.uk
Book design © 2024 Joseph Chittenden

All the images in this guide were produced by JC3DVIS.
Contains Ordnance Survey data © Crown copyright and
database right 2024

With special thanks to:
Jane Chittenden

Legal disclaimer
Neither the author nor the publisher shall be held liable or
responsible to any person or entity with respect to any loss
or incidental or consequential damages caused, or alleged to
have been caused, directly or indirectly, by the information
contained herein.

Milton Keynes UK
Ingram Content Group UK Ltd.
UKHW051018130824
446717UK00011B/85